QUICK AND EASY 5 INGREDIENT MEALS

75 Simple Homemade Recipes with 5 Ingredients or Less

LISA WEBSTER

ISBN-13: 978-1534878204

ISBN-10: 1534878203

DEDICATION

To all who love good food and want to have it as quickly as possible.

TABLE OF CONTENTS

INTRODUCTION

I once had a neighbor named Martha who spent hundreds of dollars ordering meals for her family. I noticed her kids deliberately came around my home during dinners and to their delight, I always invited them to join at the table. Her husband would rather eat out but she kept ordering despite her family's lack of interest in the meals she provided.

One day, I went over to her place with the intention of finding out what was really going on in her kitchen. I discovered she had a whole lot of wasted packed food about to be thrown away. When I asked her why she orders them even when members of her family don't seem interested in the meals, she lamented "Oh Lisa, what else can I do? I just can't bring myself to another difficult task of cooking after a hard day's work. Most times I get home late and tired. I just have to put different meals on the table each day, and you know how stressful cooking can be. I also have a lot of other things to attend to before the day runs out".

From that day, she became my first project. I made a promise to teach her a simple meal every day. I made her understand that cooking could be fun and to also know that putting a simple meal together every day need not take lots of ingredients and plenty of time. By the end of the second month after I embarked on this assignment, mealtimes in her home became something she and her family always longed for.

My neighbor is not alone in this. Thousands of working-class people go through this every day. They are either spending so much time in the kitchen after a busy day, processing and preparing so many ingredients for one meal or spending so much on food or food ingredients. Some don't even know what meal to prepare.

As a housewife who have been cooking for years and have mastered the art, I have resolved to help so many Marthas out there with my 5 ingredient recipe cookbook, bringing back the joy of mealtimes in many homes.

Each recipe is simple and fast to prepare and have an incredibly delicious result. With only five ingredients or less, you don't have to spend much money on purchasing food items or much time preparing them. Most of the ingredients used in this book are available in almost any grocery store and can be bought ahead. You no longer need to spend a lot of hours in the kitchen trying to prepare one meal that would be eaten in a few minutes and forgotten; spend large amount of money ordering your meals when you get home late from work; spend time thinking about what to cook for the next meal and look for scarce ingredients that are hardly available.

The cooking methods used in this book are easy to follow and the equipment and utensils are simple and can be found in every kitchen- pots, baking dishes and sheets, ovens, grills, microwaves, Dutch ovens, skillets, skillets, blenders, food processors etc. You don't need to acquire any special machine or equipment for any recipe in this book.

This book contains a wide variety of recipes– soups, main dishes, desserts, appetizers, side dishes and drinks– to choose from. These cooking recipes will transform your cooking experience and will turn you into a mini-cooking pro!

You are about to begin a whole new journey of delight in cooking! Fasten your seat belts, and get ready for a journey you will live to remember.

MAIN DISH RECIPES

Scrumptious Pork Chops

Everyone will ask for more of this.

Preparation: 5 minutes

Cooking time: 30 minutes

Servings: 4

Ingredients:

4 pork chops, boneless

¼ cup soy sauce

2 cups salad dressing

Pepper, to taste

Directions:

1. In a medium bowl, combine soy, salad dressing and pepper. Mix well.

2. Heat a skillet on medium heat and place the pork chops in it. Pour the soy sauce mixture over the pork chops.

3. Cover the skillet and cook on medium heat for 25 minutes. Turn every 7-8 minutes.

4. After 25 minutes, remove the lid, reduce to low heat and cook for another 5 minutes.

Chicken Pesto

A simple Italian way to prepare chicken. Best served with pasta or with a salad.

Preparation: 10 minutes

Cooking time: 25 minutes

Servings: 4

Ingredients:

4 chicken breast halves, boneless, skinless

8 tablespoons of already prepared basil pesto

4 or more slices prosciutto

Directions:

1. Heat your oven to 400°F.

2. Oil the baking pan.

3. Smear on top of each breast, 2 tablespoons of pesto.

4. Wrap-up each breast in slices of prosciutto till they are completely covered and place them in the oiled baking pan.

5. Place in the heated oven for about 25 minutes. Remove when prosciutto appears crisp and chicken is well cooked.

Lemon Grilled Spicy Shrimp

Deliciously grilled shrimp with a lemon base.

Preparation: 25 minutes

Cooking time: 5 minutes

Servings: 4

Ingredients:

3 tablespoons of lemon juice

1 tablespoon of cooking oil

About 40 medium sized shrimps (deveined and peeled)

3 tablespoons of Cajun seasoning

Directions:

1. Prepare a marinade of lemon juice, Cajun seasoning and cooking oil in a plastic bag.

2. Put the shrimp into the mixture and remove any excess air before sealing the bag.

3. Leave in the refrigerator for about 20 minutes.

4. Oil the grates of an outdoor grill and preheat to medium heat.

5. Remove the marinade coated shrimp from the bag and cook on the heated grill.

6. Cook the shrimps for about 2 minutes on each side and remove from grill when they are pink and well cooked.

Grilled Chicken With Bacon And Rosemary

A very simple way to prepare grilled chicken with the wonderful flavor and aroma of rosemary.

Preparation: 10 minutes

Cooking time: 16 minutes

Servings: 4

Ingredients:

4 chicken breast halves, skinless, boneless

4 big slices of bacon

4 teaspoons of garlic powder

4 sprigs of fresh rosemary

salt and pepper to taste

Directions:

1. Oil the grates of an outdoor grill and preheat to medium-high heat.

2. Season a chicken breast half with salt, pepper and 1 teaspoon garlic powder.

3. Place a rosemary sprig on the chicken, wrap the bacon around it to secure the rosemary on the chicken.

4. Hold the wrap firm with a tooth pick or a rosemary stem.

5. Cook the chicken breasts on the grill for 8 minutes on each side. When properly cooked, the center is no longer pink and should read at least 165°F. Remove toothpicks or rosemary stem before serving.

Baked Bacon Chicken

This tangy baked bacon chicken magic is best served with French fries or macaroni and cheese, if desired.

Preparation: 15 minutes

Cooking time: 45 minutes

Servings: 4

Ingredients:

4 chicken breast halves, skinless, boneless

16 ounces of sliced bacon

18 ounces of honey barbecue sauce

Directions:

1. Heat your oven to 350°F.

2. Wash and dry chicken then put them in a baking pan.

3. Cover the chicken with 9 ounces of barbecue sauce, then place the slices of bacon across the chicken.

4. Pour the remaining 9 ounce of barbecue sauce on it.

5. Bake for about 45 minutes at 350°F until the chicken is well cooked and the top pieces of bacon are crispy.

6. Ready to serve.

Simple Fish Bake

A simple way to bake fish, an you don't even need a sauce for it.

Preparation: 15 minutes

Cooking time: 20 minutes

Servings: 4

Ingredients:

4 salmon steaks (6 ounce each)

9 teaspoons of Dijon mustard

9 teaspoons of honey

1 teaspoons of lemon juice

Pepper to taste

Directions:

1. Heat your oven to 325°F.

2. Mix the honey, lemon juice and mustard in a bowl.

3. Smear each salmon steak with the mixture and sprinkle pepper on them.

4. Place the steaks in a baking pan.

5. Bake in the hot oven for 20 minutes until the fish appears crisp.

Romano And Pine Nuts Spaghetti Squash

A lovely meal every vegetarian should try.

Preparation: 10 minutes

Cooking time: 50 minutes

Servings: 2

Ingredients:

1 spaghetti squash, halved and seeded

4 tablespoons of toasted pine nuts

4 tablespoons of grated Romano cheese

1 tablespoon of melted butter

2 tablespoons of chopped sage

Salt and pepper to taste

Directions:

1. Heat oven to about 350°F.

2. Put the squash in a large baking pan, cut side facing down and bake in oven for 50 minutes.

3. Remove the fleshy part of the squash from outer skin with a fork and put in a bowl.

4. Include the cheese, pine nuts, butter, sage pepper and salt.

5. Stir properly and serve.

Tender Baked Onion Chicken

A tasty way to bake your chicken with a great oniony flavor. every member of the family will enjoy this.

Preparation: 5 minutes

Cooking time: 40 minutes

Servings: 3

Ingredients:

10 strips of chicken breast tenderloins

4 tablespoons of melted margarine

1 ounce of dry onion soup mix

salt and pepper to taste

Directions:

1. Heat oven to 350°F

2. Put the chicken strips in a baking pan and pour the margarine over them.

3. Add the pepper and salt and season with the onion soup mix.

4. Place in the hot oven and bake for 40 minutes until chicken is well cooked.

Basil And Tomato Salmon

An easy to prepare weeknight dinner best served with sautéed spinach.

Preparation: 10 minutes

Cooking time: 20 minutes

Servings: 2

Ingredients:

2 pieces of salmon fillets (6 ounce each)

1 thinly sliced medium sized tomato

3 teaspoons of dried basil

6 teaspoons of grated cheese

3 teaspoons of vegetable oil

Directions:

1. Heat oven to 375°F

2. Line the baking pan with aluminum foil and rub with oil to prevent the fish from sticking to it.

3. Put the salmon filets into the aluminum foil and add the basil.

4. Place the tomato slices on top and sprinkle with the vegetable oil and grated cheese.

5. Place in the heated oven for 20 minutes until salmon is well cooked and cheese turns slightly brown.

6. Ready to serve.

Cabbage With Ground Beef

A simple and special family dish. Goes well with rice, corn or cornbread.

Preparation: 15 minutes

Cooking time: 45 minutes

Servings: 4

Ingredients:

1 big sized cabbage, chopped to small pieces

3 teaspoons of Italian seasoning

1 medium sized onion, sliced thinly

ground dry black pepper and salt to taste

3 medium sized tomato, finely diced with juice

16 ounces of ground lean beef

Directions:

1. Mix the onions, cabbage, seasoning, black pepper, diced tomatoes with its juice and salt in a pot and place over low heat.

2. Crush the ground beef into the mixture while cooking gently and slowly.

3. Cover for about 45 minutes and stir every 9 minutes until the beef is thoroughly cooked and cabbage is soft.

4. Turn off heat and serve.

Chicken With Pineapple

Yummy... yummy... yummy...! You can't but try this.

Preparation: 10 minutes

Cooking time: 30 minutes

Servings: 5

Ingredients:

5 chicken breast halves, skinless, boneless

1½ ounces of dry onion soup mix

2 cups of water

15 ounces of pineapple chunks

1 large orange, sliced in rounds

3 teaspoons olive oil

Directions:

1. Oil skillet with oil spray.

2. Place the chicken breasts in the skillet with the meat side facing down.

3. Turn the chicken to the other side, add the onion soup mix, pineapple chunks and water.

4. Reduce to low heat and cover. Allow to cook gently for 30minutes.

5. Dress with the orange slices and pineapple chunks.

Baked Chicken Spinach Pesto

A great meal for people who love to eat a lot of vegetables.

Preparation: 10 minutes

Cooking time: 45 minutes

Servings: 4

Ingredients:

12 ounces of chopped spinach

6 teaspoons of grated cheese

6 teaspoons of basil pesto

4 chicken breast halves, skinless and boneless

Directions:

1. Heat an oven to 375°F.

2. Blend the basil pesto and spinach in a bowl and smear the base of a glass baking dish with half of the mixture.

3. Put the chicken breast halves into the glass dish. Pour the remaining mixture on top of the chicken.

4. Use aluminum foil to seal the dish and place in the hot oven.

5. Bake for 30 minutes until chicken is well cooked.

6. Remove foil and sprinkle with cheese. Place back in oven for another 15 minutes.

Creamy Baked Horseradish Pork Chops

A delicious and easy way to make your pork chops.

Preparation: 5 minutes

Cooking time: 45 minutes

Servings: 4

Ingredients:

4 pork chops boneless

4 tablespoons of bread crumbs

4 tablespoons of prepared horseradish

4 tablespoons of melted butter

Directions:

1. Heat oven to 350°F

2. Spray a baking pan with oil spray and put the pork chops into it.

3. Blend the bread crumbs, butter and horseradish in a separate bowl.

4. Spread each pork chop with about ¼th of the mixture to cover completely.

5. Place in the hot oven for about 45 minutes until the chops are soft.

Spicy Chili Burgers

A tasty burger recipe. Served in between burger buns with any fixing of your choice.

Preparation: 15 minutes

Cooking time: 10 minutes

Servings: 4

Ingredients:

16 ounces of ground beef

4 ounces of green chilies, diced

4 slices of Jack cheese

1 teaspoon of beef seasoning

Directions:

1. Heat your grill to a high temperature.

2. Combine the ground beef, seasoning and diced chilies in a bowl and divide into 4 flat round portions.

3. Grease the grill grate lightly.

4. Grill each round portion for 5 minutes on each side till well cooked.

5. Add cheese on top 2 minutes before removing from the grill.

Garlic And Spinach Spaghetti

A quick and great tasting dinner. Cooked chicken or fish pieces can be added when cooking, if desired.

Preparation: 5 minutes

Cooking time: 15 minutes

Servings: 4

Ingredients:

4 minced garlic cloves,

1 pound of spaghetti

3 teaspoons of vegetable oil

10 ounces of spinach, chopped

Directions:

1. Put the spaghetti into a pot of boiling water and add salt to taste. Cook for 10-12 minutes until al dente and drain.

2. Preheat the vegetable oil in a large wok.

3. Add the garlic and allow to fry for 1 minute.

4. Include the cooked spaghetti and add the spinach. Stir continually and cook for 2 more minutes.

5. Turn off heat and ready to serve.

Crispy Baked Chicken

Crispy and crunchy. Tastes just like fried chicken.

Preparation: 15 minutes

Cooking time: 45 minutes

Servings: 6

Ingredients:

6 chicken breast halves, skinless, boneless

16 ounces of soda cracker crumbs

Garlic powder to taste

1 teaspoon of salt

8 tablespoons of melted margarine

Directions:

1. Heat oven to 425°F.

2. Oil-spray a baking dish lightly.

3. Put the garlic powder salt and cracker crumbs in a bowl and mix together.

4. Immerse the chicken breast in the melted margarine and coat with cracker crumbs.

5. Arrange the crumbs coated chicken breast in the baking dish.

6. Put into the hot oven and bake for about 45 minutes until the chicken is well cooked. A thermometer should read at least 165°F when inserted in the chicken core.

Spring Veggie Pasta

A simple and great dinner, suitable for vegetarians.

Preparation: 10 minutes

Cooking time: 15 minutes

Servings: 4

Ingredients:

16 ounces of asparagus, sliced into pieces

1½ ounce of olive oil

½ pound of snap peas, sliced

8 tablespoons of grated cheese

salt and pepper to taste

½ pound of penne pasta

Directions:

1. Add a little salt to a big pot of water and boil.

2. Put the asparagus into boiling water and cook for about 2 minutes.

3. Include the peas and cook for 2 extra minutes and pour into a bowl.

4. Cook pasta in boiling water until al dente, about 10 minutes and drain.

5. Add the pasta to the bowl of peas and asparagus.

6. Mix with cheese, salt, olive oil and pepper.

SOUPS RECIPES

Chicken Broth Tomato Soup

Spice up your canned tomato soup with this recipe. Best served with sour cream and chopped rosemary, basil, parsley, cheese or croutons.

Preparation: 5 minutes

Cooking time: 15 minutes

Servings: 10 cups

Ingredients:

12 medium sized tomatoes, peeled and diced

½ teaspoon of pepper

2 pounds of chicken broth

1½ pound of undiluted canned tomato soup

Sour cream

Directions:

1. Put the diced tomatoes in a food processor and pulse until smooth.

2. Pour into a Dutch oven and add the tomato soup, pepper and chicken broth to it and stir.

3. Cook and stir every 5 minutes over medium heat for about 15 minutes.

4. Dress up with sour cream and any topping of your choice.

Cilantro Pork Posole

A simple to prepare posole yet so tasty.

Preparation: 5 minutes

Cooking time: 25 minutes

Servings: 4

Ingredients:

1 pound of pork tenderloin, cut into fine pieces

1 pound can of hominy

15 ounce can of stewed tomatoes with jalapeno peppers and spices

2 ounces of cilantro, chopped

2 teaspoons chipotle seasoning mix

1 cup of water

Directions:

1. Coat a large skillet with cooking spray and place over medium heat.

2. Sprinkle the seasoning mix on the pork pieces, stir and coat with cooking spray.

3. Put the pork into the hot skillet and cook for about 4 minutes. Add the hominy, water and canned tomato sauce and stir and leave to boil.

4. Reduce heat and allow to simmer for about 20 minutes. Add cilantro and stir.

Endive And Chicken Tomato Soup

What's more romantic than this perfect marriage of chicken, tomatoes and endive.

Preparation: 1 minute

Cooking time: 14 minutes

Servings: 4

Ingredients:

1 cups of chicken broth

2 teaspoons of vegetable oil

8 ounces of cooked chicken breast, chopped

15 ounces of canned stewed tomatoes

1 pound of endive, chopped

Directions:

1. Mix the tomatoes and broth in a large skillet and cover the mixture. Allow to boil.

2. Reduce the heat and simmer for 5 minutes. Add the endive, chicken and oil and cook for another 5 minutes.

Spinach And Sausage Barley Soup

I first tasted this soup at a friend's dinner and I made sure I left her home with the recipe. You just have to try it.

Preparation: 5 minutes

Cooking time: 18 minutes

Servings: 4

Ingredients:

8 ounces of chopped spinach

6 ounces of chicken sausage, chopped

2 ounces of easy to cook barley

15 ounces of canned stewed tomatoes

20 ounces of bell pepper stir-fry

16 ounces of water

Direction

1. Coat a large skillet with cooking spray and place over medium heat. Put the sausage into the skillet and cook until brown for about 3 minutes.

2. Blend bell pepper fry and the water in a blender until smooth. Add the stewed tomatoes, blended stir-fry and the barley to the skillet of sausage.

3. Allow the mixture to boil and then simmer for 10 minutes. Add the spinach, stir and cook for 1 more minute.

Cheese And Gnocchi Beef Soup

In just 15 minutes, you can have this great tasting soup treat on your table. You can serve with a salad.

Preparation: 1 minute

Cooking time: 14 minutes

Servings: 6

Ingredients:

1 pound of gnocchi

15 ounces of canned stewed tomatoes

4½ ounces of beef sausage

1¾ cups of beef broth

4 ounces of grated parmesan cheese

16 ounces of water

Direction:

1. Remove sausage from casing and cook in a Dutch oven over medium heat until brown, stirring at intervals.

2. Put the gnocchi, stew tomatoes, water and beef broth into a large skillet and allow to boil.

3. Turn down the heat, simmer for 5 minutes until the gnocchi begins to float.

4. Pour soup into bowls and sprinkle cheese on each serving.

Veggie Carrot Soup

One of the healthiest and easiest soups to make without canned ingredients. Just ensure that the flavoring of your stock is mild for the carrot flavor to come through.

Preparation: 5 minutes

Cooking time: 50 minutes

Servings: 10

Ingredients:

4 cups of vegetable broth

¼ cup of vegetable oil

8 big carrots, peeled

½ teaspoon of ground pepper

salt and herbs to taste

Direction:

1. Heat oven to 425F.

2. Coat carrots with 2 tablespoons of oil and place on a large baking sheet.

3. Place in hot oven for about 45 minutes. Remove when carrot edges are brown.

4. Put roasted carrots into blender, add the broth and blend. Pour the puree into a pot and bring to boil.

5. Turn down heat and add the pepper, salt and herbs. sprinkle the remaining oil on it and serve with herbs.

Cheddar Onion Potato Soup

Enjoy the rich cheesy creamy taste of Cheddar and potato combined with a sweet oniony flavor.

Preparation: 10 minutes

cooking time: 15 minutes

servings: 6

Ingredients:

3 pounds of vegetable broth

6 spring onions, chopped with green and white parts apart

½ pound of cheddar cheese, shredded

4 cups of chopped russet potatoes

6 teaspoons of Cajun seasoning

Directions:

1. Pour the broth, chopped potatoes, white part of spring onions, and the seasoning into a cooking pot. Place over medium heat, stir at intervals until it begins it boil.

2. Turn down heat and allow to simmer for 10 more minutes, stirring at intervals until potatoes become soft.

3. Remove from heat and puree using a hand blender . Add the cheese to it and stir thoroughly.

4. Pour into bowls and dress with the green part of the spring onions and some shredded cheese.

Easy Salsa Black Bean Soup

This recipe is a vegetarian delight. A healthy and satisfying soup. Can be served with any topping of your choice.

Preparation: 5 minutes

Cooking time: 20 minutes

Servings: 10

Ingredients:

16 ounces of prepared tomato salsa

8 ounces of onions, sliced

16 ounces of vegetable broth

3 teaspoons of soybeans oil

4 cups of black bean

pepper and salt to taste

Directions:

1. Put the soybeans oil in a pot over medium heat and add onions into it. Cook for 5 minutes, stirring often until soft.

2. Include the salsa, broth, salt, pepper and beans to the pot of onions and allow to boil.

3. Turn down heat immediately it starts boiling and simmer for about 15 minutes.

Simple 3 ingredient Peas and Rice Soup

A favorite in many Italian homes. Best served with grilled chicken.

Preparation: 1 minute

Cooking time: 24 minutes

Servings: 6

Ingredients:

6 cups of chicken broth

1 cup of short or long grain rice

6 ounces of frozen package peas

Direction:

1. Boil the broth in a pot and add the rice. Reduce heat and simmer for 15 minutes.

2. Hit the package peas on a hard surface to disintegrate them then add to the broth.

3. Allow to simmer for 5 minutes with the pot uncovered. Pour into serving bowl.

Broccoli Cheese Soup (Revamped)

A good way to improve the richness and taste of your canned soup.

Preparation: 5 minutes

Cooking time: 10 minutes

Servings: 6

Ingredients:

½ cup of cheddar cheese, grated

2 cans of broccoli and cheese soup

2 cups of milk

12 ounces of frozen broccoli

Directions:

1. Pour the cans of soup into a large pot and add the milk. Mix thoroughly with a hand mixer.

2. Add the broccoli and allow to cook until tender, stir at intervals. Then add almost all the cheese.

3. Serve in bowls, add pepper and salt if needed, and the rest of the cheese on top.

Easy Roasted Pumpkin Soup

Try this creamy and velvety smooth pumpkin soup, especially at holiday dinners.

Preparation: 10 minutes

Cooking time: 1 hour

Servings: 4

Ingredients:

½ cup of coconut milk

1 medium sized pumpkin

2 cups of vegetable stock

1 small can of pumpkin

½ teaspoon of ginger

Directions:

1. Heat oven to 400°F. Clean the pumpkin and place in oven for 1 hour to roast.

2. Bring out from oven, skin and seed the roasted pumpkin.

3. Put canned pumpkin, stock, coconut milk, fresh pumpkin and ginger into a blender. Blend until smooth.

SIDE DISH RECIPES

Cheese And Bacon Tater

You can vary the excitement from this tater tots side dish by using different kinds and quantities of cheese and bacon any time you make it.

Preparation: 5 minutes

Cooking time: 30 minutes

Servings: 6

Ingredients:

1 pound of tater tots

1 cup of sour cream

5 strips of bacon, cooked and cut to pieces

1 pound of cheese, shredded

2 ounces of scallions, chopped

Directions:

1. Preheat oven to 425°F. Arrange the tots in a baking pan, put in hot oven and cook for 20 minutes.

2. Line a dish with a cookie sheet and put tots in it. Sprinkle with shredded cheese and bacon pieces.

3. Place back into hot oven, uncovered for 10 minutes until all the cheese is melted.

4. Top with scallions and serve with sour cream as dipping.

Macaroni And Cheese Spinach Casserole

Creamy macaroni and cheese layered with spinach and topped with buttery breadcrumbs.

Preparation: 15 minutes

Cooking time: 35 minutes

Servings: 6

Ingredients:

½ pound of spinach, chopped

1 ounce of parmesan cheese, shredded

4¾ cups of packed macaroni and cheese

5.2 ounces of breadcrumbs

1½ ounce of melted butter

Directions:

1. Preheat oven to 350°F.

2. Grease a casserole with cooking spray.

3. Divide the macaroni and cheese and spread the first part evenly in the greased casserole. Add the spinach to cover the macaroni and cheese. Top the spinach with the second part of the macaroni and cheese.

4. Mix the cheese, butter and breadcrumbs in a small bowl. Sprinkle the mixture on over the casserole.

5. Place in the hot oven and bake until crumbs are turning brown at most 35 minutes.

Easy Cheesy Bacon Baked Potato

A unique side dish with a cheesy bacon stuffing.

Preparation: 5 minutes

Cooking time: 18 minutes

Servings: 4

Ingredients:

2 ounces of bacon, cut into pieces

4 medium sized potatoes, baked

½ cup of cream cheese

1 teaspoon of red pepper

6 ounces of shredded cheddar cheese

Directions:

1. Heat oven to 400°F.

2. Cut the potatoes, lengthwise into four and scrape out the middle leaving about ½ inch of potato.

3. Mix the bacon bits, pepper, cheddar and cream cheese thoroughly to form a thick mixture

4. Place firmly on each potato skin and put into hot oven for 15 minutes to bake.

5. Broil tops until they are light brown for about 3 minutes.

Tomato Cheese Asparagus

This meal tell the story of Spring, "freshness". Very lovely, especially if the Parmesan and asparagus are as fresh as possible.

Preparation: 5 minutes

Cooking time: 12 minutes

Servings: 4

Ingredients:

4 tablespoons of Parmesan cheese, grated

16 ounces of fresh asparagus

6 teaspoons of vegetable oil

5.2 ounces of water

10 medium sized tomatoes, halved

Directions:

1. Put the asparagus in a cooking pan over medium heat add the water and cover. Allow to boil for 10 minutes until soft.

2. Drain off water, return the cooking pan to heat and turn down heat to low.

3. Add the tomatoes to the asparagus and sprinkle with vegetable oil and cheese and cover.

4. Allow to cook for 2 minutes until the tomatoes are steamed and cheese melted.

Easy Cream Fruit Salad

A blend of mixed fruits and cream, ready in just 5 minutes. you can vary the blend of fruits or add more as desired.

Preparation: 5 minutes

Servings: 6

Ingredients:

8 ounces of grated coconut

1½ cups of peeled and separated mandarins

2½ cups of pineapple chunks

1 cup of sour cream

8 ounces of marshmallows

Directions:

1. Mix all four fruits gently together in a bowl.

2. Fold mixed fruits into sour cream.

3. Ready to serve. Refrigerate for later use.

Quick And Easy Roasted Garlic And Broccoli

Crisp tender broccoli seasoned with garlic and pepper.

Preparation: 5 minutes

Cooking time: 20 minutes

Servings: 4

Ingredients:

1 ounce of vegetable oil

24 ounces of broccoli, sliced

½ cup of garlic, sliced

salt and pepper to taste

Directions:

1. Heat oven to 450°F.

2. Spread the broccoli on a baking sheet. Sprinkle the salt, garlic, vegetable oil and pepper on it.

3. Roast in hot oven for 20 minutes until crispy. Ready to serve.

Simple Oven Baked Polenta

Enjoy this oven baked polenta with roasted pork and vegetables.

Preparation: 5 minutes

Cooking time: 30 minutes

Servings: 6

Ingredients:

4 tablespoons of olive oil

1 pound of package polenta

8 cups of water

½ teaspoon of salt

Directions:

1. Heat oven to 350°Fs.

2. Spray oil spay on a baking pan and line with parchment paper.

3. Boil the water in a large pot and add salt and olive oil. Turn down heat when boil and stir in polenta for 3 minutes until smooth and thick.

4. Pour the polenta evenly in the prepared pans, place in hot oven and bake for 20 minutes.

5. Remove from heat and allow to cool. Cut into shapes and serve.

Onion Spinach Sauté

A great side dish for vegetarians. Best served while it's still warm.

Preparation: 10 minutes

Cooking time: 10 minutes

Servings: 2

Ingredients:

3 teaspoons of soybeans oil

12 ounce of baby spinach

1 small onion, chopped

3 teaspoons of butter

black pepper and salt to taste

Directions:

1. Place a saucepan over heat and add butter to melt. Add the oil and onions to melted butter and fry for 3 minutes until soft.

2. Stir in spinach and cook until wilted. Put in pepper and salt and mix gently.

3. Ready to serve.

Corn In Milk Side Dish

Try this fried corn served on toast and you will be pleased.

Preparation: 5 minutes

Cooking time: 10 minutes

Servings: 6

Ingredients:

4 teaspoons of corn flour

1 ounce of onions, chopped

1½ teaspoons of bacon fat

1¾ cup of processed corn

8 ounces of milk

Directions:

1. Place a saucepan over heat and add bacon fat to melt.

2. Put the onions into it and allow to fry. Stir in the corn flour and add the milk and corn. Stir thoroughly.

3. Ready to serve.

Buttered Braised Turnips

Deliciously braised turnips with a sweet buttery taste.

Preparation: 5 minutes

Cooking time: 30 minutes

Servings: 4

Ingredients:

1½ ounce of lemon juice

1½ ounce of butter

15 small white turnips

1 ounce of maple syrup

salt to taste

Directions:

1. Preheat a saucepan for 5 minutes over medium heat. Put 1 ounce of butter in the saucepan and allow to melt.

2. Cut turnips lengthwise into 2 and place them cut side facing downwards in the saucepan. Fry for 4 minutes without turning until it turns golden.

3. Add the lemon juice, salt and about 2 cups of water and boil.

4. Turn down heat, cover and simmer for 5 minutes until tender. Remove cover and turn up heat again, allow to boil for 4 minutes until almost dry. Cook for another 8 minutes stirring often until all liquid has evaporated.

5. Add the ½ ounce of butter and maple syrup and stir.

Crispy Okra Fries

Crunchy, crispy, creamy deliciously fried smashed okra.

Preparation: 15 minutes

Cooking time: 25 minutes

Servings: 6

Ingredients:

1 pound of cornmeal

16 ounces of okra

12 ounces of buttermilk

1 cup of vegetable oil

pepper and salt to taste

Directions:

1. Beat the okra with a meat mallet from the tip to the stem end.

2. Put the cornmeal and buttermilk into 2 separate dishes. Add salt and pepper into the cornmeal and stir.

3. Dip the smashed okra into the buttermilk and coat with coat with cornmeal.

4. Heat a Dutch oven to 350°F and pour the oil into it. Fry the okra about 1½ minutes on each side until crisp brown. Remove from heat and drain using paper towels.

5. Do this in batches until all have been fried. Sprinkle with pepper and salt as desired and serve.

Grilled Cheese And Corn Salad

A popular Mexican dish. Corn and cheese with a zest of lemon.

Preparation: 5 minutes

Cooking time: 15 minutes

Servings: 6

Ingredients:

2.6 ounces of chives, sliced

¼ cup of lemon juice

5.2 ounces of white cheese, crumbled

8 big corn on cob

1½ ounces of mayonnaise

Directions:

1. Heat grill to 450°F.

2. Coat corn with mayonnaise and sprinkle pepper and salt on it. Grill for about 12 minutes, turning until all sides are cooked.

3. Remove grains from cob into a bowl. Add cheese, lemon juice and chives to corn and stir.

Easy Grilled Squash With Salsa Verde

A very interesting Spanish vegetable side dish. Home-grilled squash with freshly prepared salsa Verde. Try it.

Preparation: 5 minutes

Cooking time: 10 minutes

Servings: 6

Ingredients:

5 medium sized squash

8 ounces of pumpkin seed, shelled, toasted

Salsa Verde

4 tablespoons of crumbled feta cheese

1½ ounce of vegetable oil

Directions:

1. Heat your grill to 350°F.

2. Slice the squash vertically and 0.25 inch slices and coat slices with vegetable oil and a sprinkle of salt.

3. Grill for 10 minutes until it turns dark brown.

4. Remove from grill and sprinkle the toasted pumpkin seeds, crumbled feta cheese and salsa Verde.

Zucchini And Bell Pepper Tortellini

This is a unique pasta salad. You can add other grilled vegetables to make it richer.

Preparation: 5 minutes

Cooking time: 20 minutes

Servings: 6

Ingredients:

8 ounces of mini sweet bell peppers, seeded

8 ounces of lemon based Vinaigrette

2½ cups of packed tortellini

3 medium sized zucchini, halved lengthwise

8 ounces of basil leaves

Directions:

1. Heat grill to about 400°F.

2. Mix gently the zucchini and bell pepper with salt and pepper to taste.

3 Place on hot grill and allow to grill for 5 minutes per side until soft. Remove and chop roughly after cooling for 5 minutes.

4. Cook the tortellini for about 10 minutes. Add the vinaigrette, salt and pepper to taste and the grilled zucchini and pepper. Toss lightly.

5. Add the basil leaves on top and serve.

Corn And Cream Salad

A very fast to make corn salad, made without cooking.

Preparation: 25 minutes

Servings: 3

Ingredients:

18 ounces of fresh corn grains

8 tablespoons of whipped cream

salt and black pepper to taste

Directions:

1. Put 8 ounces of corn into a food processor and blend for about 1 minute until creamy.

2. Mix the rest of the corn grains (10 ounces) with the corn paste in a bowl and add salt and pepper.

3. Fold whipped cream in corn mixture. Allow to stand for 15 minutes and stir.

4. You can serve immediately or within 2 hours of preparation.

DESSERT

Creamy Grilled Pound Cake Sandwich

You have to try this grilled pound cakes. Pound cakes have never tasted so great, especially with sweetened whipped cream.

Preparation: 5 minutes

Cooking time: 5 minutes

Servings: 4

Ingredients:

8 thick slices of pound cake

¼ cup of cream cheese

8 tablespoons of whipped cream

4 medium sized strawberries

Directions:

1. Coat one side of the cake slice with 1 tablespoon of cream cheese and top with another slice. Do same with the remaining slices of pound cake and cream cheese.

2. Grill the pound cake at 400°F and cover grill. Turn to the other side after 2½ minutes.

3. Remove from grill and top each grilled cake with 2 tablespoons of whipped cream and a berry.

Chocolate And Coconut Macaroons

These macaroons are very easy to make but will simply blow your taste buds away.

Preparation: 5 minutes

Cooking time: 20 minutes

Servings: 12

Ingredients:

12 tablespoons of condensed milk

½ teaspoon of almond extract

24 unblanched almonds

14 ounces of coconuts, flaked

4 ounces of chocolate morsels

1 pinch of salt

Directions:

1. Mix the condensed milk, almond extract, flaked coconuts and salt in a bowl.

2. Line a baking sheet with aluminum foil and scoop out the mixture unto the foil using a greased tablespoon. Place an almond on top of each cookie.

3. Bake in an oven for about 17 minutes at 350°F. Remove when golden and allow to cool.

4. Put the chocolate morsels in a microwaveable bowl and microwave at high until completely melted for 75 seconds, stirring every 30 seconds.

5. Pour melted chocolate into a sealable plastic bag, pierce the bottom corner of the bag and pipe the chocolate over the cookies by squeezing the bag gently.

Vanilla Chocolate Soufflés

Great dessert recipe for family dinners and dinner parties.

Preparation: 10 minutes

Cooking time: 20 minutes

Servings: 4

Ingredients:

6 teaspoons of brown sugar

½ tablespoon of vanilla extract

4 ounces of semisweet chocolate chips

1 tablespoon of butter

4 eggs

2.6 ounces of jam, seedless

Directions:

1. Oil the sides and bottom of 4 stainless steel measuring cups with butter then sprinkle with sugar until both sides and bottom of the greased cups are sugar coated.

2. Put the chocolate chips and jam in a microwaveable bowl and place in microwave at medium heat for 90 seconds until melted. Stir at 30 second intervals. Remove from microwave, pour in the vanilla and stir.

3. Break the eggs and remove the yolk. Whisk the egg white with an electric mixer at high speed. Pour a third of the egg white into the chocolate mixture and stir.

4. Fold the mixture into the egg white then spoon into the stainless steel cups evenly. Wipe clean and make a small indentation around the edges of the cups with the tip of your thumb.

5. Place cups on a baking sheet and bake for 20 minutes at 350°F until soufflés rises and becomes brown.

Snow Berry Pud

This is a lovely fat-free dessert recipe. Other kinds of berries can also be used instead of strawberry.

Preparation: 15 minutes

Freezing time: 2 hours 15 minutes

Servings: 6

Ingredients:

26½ ounces of strawberries

1 medium sized lemon, juice

5 ounces of sugar

Directions:

1. Remove hull and chop the strawberries. Put in a large bowl with the lemon juice and sugar.

2. Pour about 1½ cup of boiling water into the mixture and leave to macerate and cool. Turn into a food processor and process until smooth, then sieve.

3. Pour into a sided metal tray and cover the tray with cling film. Place in the freezer for about 45 minutes until the edges become frozen. Break the ice with a fork into tiny crystals and return into freezer. Repeat the process of breaking the ice at least 3 times after 30 minutes intervals until the texture is that of snow.

Coconut Almond Bars

An easy to carry snack that can be eaten on-the-go and great as dessert.

Preparation: 10 minutes

refrigeration: 30 minutes

Servings: 4

Ingredients:

4 ounces of coconut, flaked

2 ounces of cashew

2.6 ounces of almonds, slivered

10 dates, pitted

1 teaspoon of coconut oil

Directions:

1. Process the almond and coconut in a food processor. Include the dates and pulse until well mixed, then include the coconut oil and cashew until thick and the mixture sticks together.

2. Pour on a sheet of waxed paper, make into a bar and wrap with the waxed paper by folding the sides on top.

3. Refrigerate for 30 minutes until solid.

Watermelon And Mint Soup

This cold soup is a refreshing dessert on a hot afternoon.

Preparation: 15 minutes

Refrigeration: 2 hours

Servings: 4

Ingredients:

2 pounds of watermelon, seeded and cubed

3 teaspoons of mint, chopped

1 small lemon, juiced

3 teaspoons of honey

Directions:

1. Put the lemon juice, watermelon, honey and mint into a blender and blend until smooth.

2. Refrigerate for 2 hours and serve.

Baked Cream Pears

A very simple to make dessert with a highly creamy delicious taste.

Preparation: 10 minutes

Cooking time: 30 minutes

Servings: 4

Ingredients:

6 teaspoons of sugar

8 tablespoons of whipping cream

6 teaspoons of butter

2 Bosc pears, halved

Directions:

1. Heat oven to 375°F.

2. Oil a baking dish with 3 teaspoons of butter and coat dish with 3 teaspoons of sugar.

3. Spread the remaining 3 teaspoons of butter on the pear halves and place the cut pear facing downwards in the sugar coated dish.

4. Sprinkle the remaining sugar on the pear halves and place in hot oven for 10 minutes.

5. Remove and pour the whipping cream on the pear, place back in oven and bake for another 20 minutes.

Easy Melt Homemade Chocolate

A healthy and homemade chocolate. They melt easily in the mouth and have no artificial ingredients.

Preparation: 10 minutes

Refrigeration: 1 hour

Servings: 6

Ingredients:

8 tablespoons of cocoa butter

½ teaspoon of liquid vanilla

1½ ounces of honey

8 tablespoons of cocoa powder

Directions:

1. Melt the cocoa butter over medium heat in a frying pan.

2. Add the cocoa powder, vanilla and honey into it and stir until properly mixed.

3. Pour the mixture into a chocolate mold and refrigerate for about an hour.

Cinnamon Apple Bake

Crunchy baked apple slices with a cinnamon glaze.

Preparation: 5 minutes

Cooking time: 15 minutes

Servings: 2

Ingredients:

1 medium sized apple, peeled, cored, sliced

3 teaspoons of flour

1 pinch of cinnamon powder

4 teaspoons of sugar

1/8 cup of water

Directions:

1. Heat oven to 350°F

2. Place the sliced apples in a baking pan. Mix the flour and water together in a bowl and pour on the apple slices.

3. Stir gently and sprinkle the cinnamon and sugar on the sliced apple.

4. Put into hot oven and cook for 15 minutes until apples are soft.

Creamy Peanut Butter Banana Ice

This is a great ice cream for vegetarians. Water or milk can be used instead of yogurt. Serve with fruits or whipped cream.

Preparation: 10 minutes

Freezing time: 2 hours

Servings: 2

Ingredients:

2 very ripe bananas, sliced

2 drops of liquid vanilla

2 teaspoons of peanut butter

1 teaspoon of sugar

1 teaspoon of yogurt

Directions:

1. Put the slices of banana in a bowl and freeze for about 2 hours until frozen.

2. Put the frozen bananas, yogurt, sugar and vanilla into a blender and blend until creamy.

3. Add the peanut butter and blend further until very smooth.

Walnut And Raisin Cookies

This cookie recipe is a family delight and has been passed from one generation to the other.

Preparation: 10 minutes

Cooking time: 10 minutes

Servings: 10

Ingredients:

2 eggs, whisked

8 ounces of raisins

12 ounces of walnuts, chopped

8 tablespoons of cooking oil

2¼ cups of spice cake mix

Directions:

1. Heat oven to 350°F.

2. Put the eggs, oil and cake mix in a bowl and mix to form a batter. Add the walnuts and raisins by folding in the batter.

3. Spoon large tablespoonful of the batter into a baking sheet, place in hot oven and bake for about 10 minutes.

Simple Homemade Peanut Brittle

Crunchy peanut brittles. I love serving mine with bananas.

Preparation: 10 minutes

Cooking time: 5 minutes

Refrigeration: 30 minutes

Servings: 4

Ingredients:

8 ounces of peanuts, shelled

8 ounces of sugar

1 ounce of shortening

½ teaspoon of salt

Directions:

1. Line a baking sheet or metal tray with wax paper.

2. Melt the shortening in a pan over medium heat and add the salt and sugar to it. Stir till dissolved totally and remove from heat.

3. Coat the peanuts with the melted mixture by stirring completely in it. Spread the coated peanuts on the wax paper lined tray or sheet.

4. Refrigerate for about 30 minutes, remove from wax paper and break to pieces.

APPETIZER

Walnut And Cinnamon Balls

A great tasting raw food snack. Try it.

Preparation: 10 minutes

Servings: 2

Ingredients:

4 ounces of walnuts

1½ ounces of ground cinnamon

5 pitted dates

1 teaspoon of cardamom powder

3 teaspoons of chopped walnuts

Directions:

1. Mix the ground cinnamon, cardamom, dates and walnuts in a blender.

2. Roll the mixture into small balls.

3. Coat the balls with the chopped walnuts by rolling the ball over the chopped walnuts.

5. Place in refrigerator.

Pepperoni Bagel Pizzas

An easy way to make your pizzas on a mini bagel.

Preparation: 10 minutes

Cooking time: 10 minutes

Servings: 4

Ingredients:

4 tablespoons of pizza sauce

16 slices of pepperoni

4 mini bagels, sliced in two

5½ tablespoons of grated pizza blend cheese

Directions:

1. Heat oven to 425°F.

2. Line your baking pan with aluminum foil and place the mini bagels on it, the cut sides facing up.

3. Spread the pizza sauce on the bagel halves and then the pizza cheese.

4. Put 2 slices of pepperoni on top of each bagel.

5. Place in the hot oven and bake for about 8 minutes when the cheese is melted and the pepperoni is light brown.

Yogurt Lemon Dip

A great recipe for dipping fruits.

Preparation: 10 minutes

Servings: 2

Ingredients:

12 ounces of yogurt

2.6 ounces of granulated sucralose

2 ounces of lemon juice

Directions:

1. Mix the lemon juice, yogurt and sucralose and lemon zest together in a bowl and refrigerate.

Fluffy Angel Spread

This is a great family hit. Nice on bread or bagels.

Preparation: 10 minutes

Servings: 4

Ingredients:

16 ounces of softened butter

1 teaspoon of liquid vanilla

8 tablespoons of sugar

1 teaspoon of cinnamon powder

8 tablespoons of honey

Directions:

1. Whisk butter, cinnamon, sugar, vanilla and honey in a bowl using an electric mixer for about 3 minutes until very soft and light.

Hard-Cooked Eggs

The best method of making hard steamed eggs. The eggs are firm and easily peeled.

Preparation: 5 minutes

Cooking time: 15 minutes

Post cooking: 20 minutes

Servings: 8

Ingredients:

8 raw eggs

Directions:

1. Insert a steamer into a pot of water, with the water just below the steamer. Heat until water is almost boiled.

2. Place eggs into the steamer and steam for 15 minutes.

3. Remove from steamer and immediately put in ice and water, make a small crack at the flat end the eggs and leave them in the iced water for 20 minutes.

4. Peel and serve.

Pecan Ranch Cheeseball

A quick and easy to make appetizer. Lovely on crackers.

Preparation: 15 minutes

Servings: 2

Ingredients:

3 teaspoons of Greek yogurt

4 tablespoons of ground pecans

2 table spoons of ranch dressing mix

1 cup of shredded Cheddar cheese

1 cup of cream cheese

Directions:

1. Mix yogurt and dressing mix in a bowl until smooth.

2. Include the cream and cheddar cheese and blend thoroughly with hands.

3. Place the mixture in a refrigerator for 5 minutes, remove and make into a ball.

4. Put the pecans in a tray. Coat the cheese ball with pecans by rolling it on the pecans.

5. ready to serve.

Avocado And Cheese Toast

Great idea for bread, especially when low on ingredients. The avocado should be fresh and ripe for best results.

Preparation: 10 minutes

Cooking time: 5 minutes

Servings: 2

Ingredients:

1 medium sized avocado pear, peeled and sliced

1/8 pound of Cheddar cheese, sliced into 8

2 slices of bread

Directions:

1. Heat oven to 300°F.

2. Put sliced bread in a baking pan and place 4 slices of cheese on each.

3. Place in the hot oven and bake for 5 minutes.

4. Cover with avocado slices.

Cream Cheese Wonton Wraps

This cheesy wonton wraps are quick and easy to make. They are great snacks and appetizers.

Preparation: 15 minutes

Cooking time: 5 minutes

Servings: 4

Ingredients:

12 teaspoons of cream cheese

½ tablespoon of water

12 wonton wraps

½ tablespoon of vegetable oil

Directions:

1. Heat oven to 400°F.

2. Grease a baking sheet with the cooking oil and place wonton wraps on sheet.

3. put 1 teaspoon of the cheese in the middle of each wonton wrap.

4. Brush the edges of the wraps lightly with water and fold in 2 in a triangle.

5. Seal the edges of the wraps by pressing them together. Raise the tips of each triangle so that they meet at the center then press to seal.

6. Brush the wrapped wontons lightly with vegetable oil.

7. Place in hot oven and bake for about 5 minutes until wontons are golden and crispy.

Chocolate Bacon Strips

Great combination of the saltiness of bacon and the sweetness tasting chocolate. Always preserve in a refrigerator.

Preparation:10 minutes

Cooking time: 20 minutes

Post cooking: 30 minutes

Servings: 6

Ingredients:

12 thick bacon strips

8 ounces of semisweet chocolate chips

1 tablespoon of butter

12 wooden skewers

Directions:

1. Heat oven to 400°F and put a wide baking sheet beneath a baking rack.

2. Put a skewer though each bacon strips and place and on baking rack.

3. Place skewered bacon in the hot oven and bake for about 20 minutes until crisp. Remove from heat and cool.

4. Mix the butter and chocolate chips in a microwavable bowl and heat in microwave stirring every 30 seconds until mixture is smooth and melted.

5. Spread the chocolate mixture over each side of the bacon using a pastry brush.

6. Place in paraffin paper and refrigerate for 30 minutes until firm.

Delicious Black Beans Hummus

This delicious hummus is a great replacement for meat in sandwiches. You can replace the lime with lemon juice and add other spices as you wish.

Preparation: 10 minutes

Servings: 4

Ingredients:

15 ounce of already prepared black beans

2 teaspoons of lime juice

1 teaspoon of ground garlic

3 teaspoons of dried basil

Directions:

1. Put the black beans, garlic, lice and basil into a food processor and blend for about 10 minutes or until thick.

Bacon And Cheddar Pulls

This delicious recipe is a good complement for a variety of foods and a great appetizer for parties.

Preparation: 10 minutes

Cooking time: 30 minutes

Servings: 4

Ingredients:

3 bacon strips

1 cup of grated Cheddar cheese

16 ounce loaf of sourdough bread

3 teaspoons of dry ranch seasoning mix

4 ounces of melted butter

Directions:

1. Heat oven to 350°F.

2. Put the bacon strips into a skillet and cook for 5 minutes on medium heat stirring often it is cooked half-cooked.

3. Dry the bacon with a paper towel. Slice the bacon crosswise into small pieces.

4. Make a checkerboard pattern on the bread by creating slits halfway through the bread, horizontally and vertically. Insert the bacon and cheese pieces into the cuts.

5. Combine the utter and dressing mix in a bowl and stir. Put the mixture over the cut bread and allow to drain into slits.

6. Use aluminum foil to wrap the whole loaf and place in a baking pan. Place in hot oven to bake for 15 minutes.

7. Remove wrapper and place back into oven. Bake for another 10 minutes until bacon becomes crisp and all the cheese melted.

DRINKS

Simple Ginger Beer With Lemon Margaritas

You wouldn't want to make any other margarita once you try this one. You can line the outer rim of the serving glass with lime and kosher salt.

Preparation: 5 minutes

Servings: 1

Ingredients:

2 tablespoons of fresh lemon juice

6 tablespoons of ginger beer

1 tablespoon of agave syrup

3 Tablespoons of agave tequila

½ cup of ice

Directions:

1. Put the ginger beer, agave syrup, lemon juice and tequila into a cocktail shaker, with some ice and mix thoroughly without covering.

2. Pour the ginger beer mixture into a serving glass and add some ice cubes in it. Slip a lime wedge on the rim of the glass and serve.

Maca And Bananas In Soymilk Shake

Simple, flavorful, so delicious yet healthy drink.

Preparation: 5 minutes

Servings: 2

Ingredients:

1 cup of soymilk

3 teaspoons of simple syrup

1 pound of frozen chopped bananas

1 teaspoon liquid vanilla

1 ounce of maca root powder

Directions:

1. place the soymilk, bananas, simple syrup, maca powder and vanilla into a blender and blend until smooth.

Yellow-Sun Punch

This is a great drink, cool and refreshing, for birthday parties, summer gathering or outdoor picnics.

Preparation: 10 minutes

Servings: 16

Ingredients:

6 ounce of orange juice concentrate

67 ounces of lime flavored soda

5¾ cups of pineapple juice

Directions:

1. Pour the orange concentrate and pineapple juice into a pitcher and mix thoroughly.

2. Add the soda gradually to allow the frizz settle. Put into a freezer and free overnight.

3. Thaw for at least 2 hours to become slushy before serving.

Chocolate Crackers And Marshmallow Milkshake

You can use chocolate hazelnut spread instead of peanut butter for this great treat. Top with crumbs and pieces of crackers and some marshmallows.

Preparation: 10 minutes

Servings: 2

Ingredients:

24 ounces of vanilla ice cream

4 big sized toasted marshmallows

2 sheets of graham crackers

4 tablespoons of chocolate peanut butter

8 ounces of milk

Directions:

1. Blend the milk and ice cream in a blender until velvety. Add the crackers, marshmallows and peanut butter into it and pulse.

2. Serve chilled.

Strawberry Ice Lemonade

A quick and easy way to cool-off in a hot sunny afternoon.

Preparation: 2 minutes

Servings: 2

Ingredients:

4 tablespoons of honey

8 tablespoons of strawberries, chopped

16 ounces of seltzer water

8 ounces of lemon juice

6 teaspoons of mint leaves

Directions:

1. Mix the mint leaves, honey and strawberries in a shaker. Squash with a ladle.

2. Include the seltzer and lemon juice and serve in a glass of ice.

Spinach And Chocolate Banana Smoothie

Who would ever know that spinach and chocolate could combine to form a delicious delight.

Preparation: 5 minutes

Servings: 1

Ingredients:

8 ounces of spinach

8 ounces of chocolate almond milk

1 frozen banana, chopped

4 tablespoons of yogurt

¼ teaspoon ground cinnamon.

Directions:

1. Mix the spinach, bananas, chocolate milk and yogurt together in a blender until creamy.

2. Serve in a glass and top with the ground cinnamon.

Green Detoxifying Coconut Juice

This is a healthy drink rich in electrolytes and potassium will help detoxify your body system.

Preparation: 5 minutes

Servings: 2

Ingredients:

8 ounce of kale

1 small sized banana

8 ounce of spinach

1 medium sized fresh coconut

Directions:

1. Crack the coconut carefully using a cleaver and pour out the water into a blender. Scrape the coconut flesh into the blender using a spoon.

2. Add the kale, bananas and spinach to the coconut and blend for 30 seconds on high speed until smooth.

3. Pour into coconut shell and serve.

Berry And Pomegranate Chia Smoothie

A wonderful way to start your morning. Very rich in antioxidants, protein, vitamin c, fiber and anti-inflammatory omega 3s and great for dieting.

Preparation: 5 minutes

Servings: 1

Ingredients:

8 ounce of pomegranate juice

1 teaspoon of chia seeds

8 ounce of assorted berries

½ cup of water

Directions:

1. Put the berries, chia seeds, pomegranate juice and water into a blender and blend until velvety smooth.

2. Sprinkle with some extra chia seed as topping (optional) and serve.

Yogurt And Mango Smoothie

Enjoy the rich taste of mango in this tropical smoothie.

Preparation: 2 minutes

Serving: 3

Ingredients:

4 cups of mango sorbet

5.2 ounces of plain yogurt

1 medium sized mango, chopped

Directions:

1. Put all the ingredients into a blender and blend until smooth.

2. Serve with chopped mango as topping.

Made in the USA
Monee, IL
17 April 2023

31999234R00052